DINOSAURS

David Burnie

KINGFISHER
NEW YORK

KINGFISHER
LONDON & NEW YORK

Copyright © Kingfisher 2010
First published in 2010 by Kingfisher
This edition published 2012 in the United States by Kingfisher,
175 Fifth Ave., New York, NY 10010
Kingfisher is an imprint of Macmillan Children's Books, London.
All rights reserved.

Illustrations by Sam and Steve Weston
Gary Hanna
Peter Bull Art Studio

Distributed in the U.S. and Canada by Macmillan, 175 Fifth Ave., New York, NY 10010

Library of Congress Cataloging-in-Publication data has been applied for.

ISBN: 978-0-7534-6862-3

Kingfisher books are available for special promotions and premiums. For details contact:
Special Markets Department, Macmillan, 175 Fifth Ave., New York, NY 10010.

For more information, please visit www.kingfisherbooks.com

Printed in China
1 3 5 7 9 8 6 4 2
1TR/0412/UTD/WKT/140MA

Note to readers: The website addresses listed in this book are correct at the time of publishing. However, due to the ever-changing nature of the Internet, website addresses and content can change. Websites can contain links that are unsuitable for children. The publisher cannot be held responsible for changes in website addresses or content, or for information obtained through third-party websites. We strongly advise that Internet searches be supervised by an adult.

The Publisher would like to thank the following for permission to reproduce their material. Every care has been taken to trace copyright holders. However, if there have been unintentional omissions or failure to trace copyright holders, we apologize and will, if informed, endeavor to make corrections in any future edition. (t = top, b = bottom, c = center, r = right, l = left):

Cover Shutterstock/DM7; and pages 8t Corbis/Jim Sugar; 9 Getty/National Geographic Society; 9b Corbis/Louie Psihoyos; 11 Corbis/Louie Psihoyos; 15 Dean Steadman/Kingfisher; 17c Corbis/Louie Psihoyos/Science Faction; 17b Natural History Museum, London; 19 Natural History Museum, London; 20 Corbis/Louie Psihoyos/Science Faction; 24 Natural History Museum, London; 26 Press Association Images; 28 Corbis/Louie Psihoyos; 32 Alamy/Friedrich Saurer; 35bl Corbis/Louie Psihoyos/Science Faction; 36 Corbis/Louie Psihoyos; 39 Getty/Dorling Kindersley; 40 Corbis/Louie Psihoyos; 42tl Science Photo Library/D. Van Ravenswway; 42cr Corbis/Michael and Patricia Fogden; 48trCorbis/Paul Vicente; 48cl Nature Picture Library/John Cancalosi; 48cr Getty/Ian Waldie; 48bl Corbis/Xinhua Photo.

CONTENTS

RULING REPTILES

Dinosaurs included the biggest land animals that have ever existed on Earth. They were reptiles—like today's snakes and lizards—but they were not the only ones alive during prehistoric times. They shared the world with many other giant reptiles, including ones that swam and ones that flew on wings made of skin. By the end of the Cretaceous Period, 65 million years ago, all of them became extinct.

Cretaceous coast

Watched by pterosaurs flying overhead, a *Lambeosaurus* herd makes its way along the coast in late Cretaceous times. The long reign of the reptiles is nearing its cataclysmic end, but for the moment, reptiles still hold sway on land, in the air, and in the sea. *Lambeosaurus* was a duck-billed dinosaur, or hadrosaur, and it fed on plants, tearing up mouthfuls with its beak-shaped jaws. Many other dinosaurs were carnivorous, using teeth, jaws, or claws to catch their prey.

On its head, Lambeosaurus had a distinctive hollow crest.

Lambeosaurus could move on its back legs alone, or on all fours.

A large crest counterbalanced the beak.

Pteranodon

Lambeosaurus

Like all pterosaurs, Pteranodon had an extralong fourth finger that held its wings open.

> **REPTILE**—*an animal with scaly skin that lays eggs or gives birth to live young*

FLYING GIANTS

When the dinosaurs were alive, pterosaurs crisscrossed the skies on leathery wings made of skin. Most had long jaws shaped like a beak, and some had bony, backward-pointing crests. The smallest pterosaurs were not much bigger than a crow, but the largest—called *Quetzalcoatlus*—had a wingspan of 33 ft. (10m), making it the largest flying animal of all time. Instead of flapping, it probably soared on outstretched wings.

Quetzalcoatlus

Using its long neck and interlocking teeth, Elasmosaurus lunged at passing fish. It belonged to a group of reptiles called plesiosaurs.

Elasmosaurus

With its streamlined body and narrow beak, Platypterygius was a typical fishlike reptile, or ichthyosaur. It gave birth to live young.

Platypterygius

Dinosaurs lived on land, but it is likely that many could swim to cross rivers or to escape from floods.

DINOSAUR AGE

The Dinosaur Age lasted more than 160 million years. During that time, dinosaurs evolved many different shapes for different ways of life. Some moved on all fours and fed on plants while others ran on their back legs and hunted living prey. There were more than 10 major groups of dinosaurs, but not all of them existed at the same time. Some of the earliest kinds died out long before the Dinosaur Age came to an end.

ceratosaurs

allosaurs

⊖ THE BIG SPLIT

Early on in their history, dinosaurs split into two different lines. Lizard-hipped dinosaurs, or saurischians, included all the meat-eating dinosaurs, as well as the enormous plant eaters called sauropods. They are shown in the main picture above in blue branches of the family tree. Bird-hipped dinosaurs, or ornithischians, were all vegetarians. They are shown in yellow in the picture above. Confusingly, the ancestors of birds were lizard-hipped.

bird-hipped

lizard-hipped

tyrannosaurs

birds

 > Dinosaurs belonged to a group of reptiles called archosaurs, which also includes modern-day reptiles and birds.

"In most cultures, dinosaurs
are the most popular
animals of all time."

James Farlow and Michael Brett-Surman
U.S. paleontologists

TRIASSIC PERIOD

Enduring presence

The Dinosaur Age started in the late
Triassic Period, about 230 million
years ago. Throughout the Jurassic
Period, about 200 to 145 million
years ago, dinosaurs dominated
life on land. During the Cretaceous
Period, some were already in
decline. Except for the ancestors of
birds, all died out at the end of the
Cretaceous, 65 million years ago.

JURASSIC PERIOD

CRETACEOUS PERIOD

www.newscientist.com/movie/dinosaurs-interactive

stegosaurs

ankylosaurs

dromaeosaurs   **sauropods**   **pachycephalosaurs**   **ceratopsians**   **ornithopods**

PALEONTOLOGY—the study of prehistoric life using fossils and other kinds of evidence

DINOSAUR REMAINS

Almost everything known about dinosaurs comes from fossilized bones. Sometimes these are found by accident, by amateur fossil hunters, but many are unearthed by scientific experts, or paleontologists, in places that are rich in fossil-bearing rocks. In some regions, hundreds of fossils are found together. The bones are often mixed up, creating bone beds or "dinosaur graveyards" that date back many millions of years.

Dragon bones

People found fossils long before the science of fossil hunting began. In China, dinosaur fossils were thought to be the bones of dragons. Ground up, they were used as a medicine. Today, China is one of the world's most important fossil-hunting regions.

Giant on show

The world's tallest dinosaur fossil is a *Giraffatitan* in Berlin's Humboldt Museum. Found in Tanzania in the early 1900s, it was not displayed until 1937 because it took so long to assemble. It towers 40 ft. (12m) high—equivalent to a four-story building.

● HOW FOSSILS FORM

Animals fossilize when their dead remains are covered by waterborne sediment or by sand. The soft parts slowly disintegrate, but the bones gradually turn to stone. More sediment builds up above the bones, burying them deep beneath the ground. Over millions of years, the rock layers may become tilted. If the rock above wears away, the fossil is then exposed.

1. Dinosaur trapped by flood

2. Body covered by water

3. Sediment covers remains

4. Fossil slowly forms and rock layers become tilted

5. Erosion exposes fossil

> The biggest dinosaur bone known is a shoulder blade from *Supersaurus*—it measures 8 ft. (2.4m) high.

Wall of bones

At the Dinosaur National Monument, in Utah, a paleontologist chips away rock to uncover a fossilized bone. This rock face contains more than 1,500 bones belonging to sauropods and other giant dinosaurs. The rock was originally river sediment, which covered up the dinosaurs when they died. The bones are jumbled up, probably because the remains were eaten by scavenging animals—mainly other dinosaurs.

Metal probes and soft brushes are used to expose fragile fossils without causing damage.

SMALL BEGINNINGS

THEROPOD—an upright dinosaur with small arms, large back legs, and hollow bones

The world's first dinosaurs appeared about 230 million years ago. At first, they were smaller than many other reptiles, but their descendants went on to become the most successful reptiles of all time. The oldest dinosaurs found so far come from Madagascar, but one of the best known was discovered in Argentina in 1991. Called *Eoraptor*, or "dawn raider," it was a fast-moving, lightweight predator only about 3 ft. (1m) long.

slender, mobile neck

Standing tall

Sprinting on its strong back legs, *Eoraptor* carries off a lizard it has just caught. With its upright stance and small arms, *Eoraptor* was very different from other reptiles, which moved with their legs sprawled out and their bodies close to the ground. *Eoraptor* was a primitive predatory dinosaur, or theropod. It died out about 225 million years ago, but theropods went on to include giants such as *Tyrannosaurus rex*—one of the biggest hunters that has ever walked the earth.

flexible hands with fingers that could grasp

Predatory dinosaurs used their teeth to grab and tear, but they could not chew.

⊝ TREASURE TROVE

Herrerasaurus skull, Valley of the Moon

Eoraptor was found in Argentina's Valley of the Moon—a desert region famous for its fossils. Another very early dinosaur, called *Herrerasaurus*, was also found here. Both dinosaurs lived about 228 million years ago, but *Herrerasaurus* was much bigger than *Eoraptor*, measuring up to 20 ft. (6m) long. The world's oldest dinosaur fossils, from Madagascar, are about 2 million years older. They were left by plant eaters that walked on all fours.

www.projectexploration.org/eoraptor.htm

tail used as counterbalance for head and neck

hingelike ankle joint let foot bend up or down

three toes made contact with the ground

"We are just a couple of steps away from the ancestor of all dinosaurs."

Paul Sereno
leader of the team that discovered Eoraptor

∨

TETRAPOD—*an animal that has a bony skeleton and four limbs or whose ancestors were four-legged*

theropods had hollow, air-filled bones, helping to reduce weight

femur, or thighbone, was the largest in the skeleton

body's center of gravity was directly above the back legs

muscles and tendons held the head high above the body

powerful muscles provided the kick needed to run fast

large rear toes provided stability when running or standing still

INSIDE A DINOSAUR

Dinosaurs were animals that went to extremes. The smallest were not much bigger than a pigeon, while the biggest may have weighed up to 100 tons—about twelve times as heavy as an African savanna elephant, the largest land animal alive today. But despite these differences, dinosaurs were all built in a similar way. Beneath their skin and muscles, they all had a tetrapod, or four-legged, skeleton. Over millions of years, the skeleton's proportions changed to suit many different ways of life.

> *Gallimimus* belonged to a group of theropods called ornithomimids, or "bird mimics."

⊖ MIDGETS AND MONSTERS

The smallest dinosaur found so far is *Microraptor*, a tiny feathered theropod just 16 in. (40cm) long. At the other extreme, the biggest dinosaurs known include *Argentinosaurus* and *Supersaurus*, both of which grew up to 130 ft. (40m) long. *Argentinosaurus* may have tipped the scales at 100 tons, making it outweigh *Microraptor* by 200,000 times. Although dinosaurs are famous for their huge proportions, they also included a large number of medium-size animals, such as *Coelophysis*. It was built for speed and agility rather than power.

Microraptor— 16 in. (40cm)

Argentinosaurus— 130 ft. (40m)

*Coelophysis—*10 ft. (3m)

sideways-pointing eyes gave a wide view of surroundings

hard-edged beak without teeth

body skin may have been scaly or covered with short feathers

Gallimimus

http://teacher.scholastic.com/activities/dinosaurs/argentinosaurus/index.htm

Life on two legs

Gallimimus was a theropod dinosaur, standing up to 13 ft. (4m) high. Like other theropods, it moved on its back legs and had small arms that ended in three-fingered hands. It had an elongated skull, with beaklike jaws. Instead of living by hunting alone, it probably fed on a mixture of plant and animal food.

hands may have been used for digging up food

scaly skin on legs

COLOR AND DISGUISE

A huge amount is known about dinosaur skeletons, but no one knows what dinosaur bodies would have looked like from the outside. Traditionally, they are often painted a plain gray, like gigantic rhinos or elephants. However, small dinosaurs—such as *Coelophysis*—may well have been brightly colored, like many lizards are today. Bold patterns would have broken up their outline, helping them blend in with their background as they stalked their prey.

Coelophysis may have had brightly colored, patterned skin that camouflaged it among the shadows of the undergrowth.

SOFT TOUCH

Living reptiles are all covered with scales. Although dinosaurs were reptiles, fossils of some species—such as *Sinosauropteryx*—show that they were covered with fine, fuzzy down. Others had simple feathers, even though they could not fly. These body coverings might have been brightly colored, helping dinosaurs attract partners when the time came to mate.

Sinosauropteryx

> Dinosaur colors were produced by chemical pigments, such as melanin, stored inside cells in their skin.

www.news.bbc.co.uk/1/hi/7124969.stm

Out of the shadows

This group of *Coelophysis* is feeding on a kill. Their markings look eye-catching in the open, but they would have worked as camouflage in sun-dappled shade. *Coelophysis* may have had different markings in males and females and another set of markings that helped adults identify their young. These juvenile markings would have changed when the young became ready to breed. Some dinosaurs may also have changed color to express their mood—a trick used by chameleons and other modern lizards.

Mummified skin

When dinosaurs died, their soft body parts usually rotted before they became fossilized. But sometimes a dinosaur's body would dry out, forming a mummified corpse. One of these "dinomummies" shows the knobbly pattern of a hadrosaur's skin in an amazing amount of detail for something over 65 million years old.

nostrils may have been high on the head or closer to the snout

chisel-shaped teeth with expanded tips tore leaves but did not chew

Brachiosaurus

GIANT PLANT EATERS

Plant-eating dinosaurs called sauropods were the largest animals ever to have walked the earth. The longest measured up to 130 ft. (40m) from head to tail and may have weighed more than 100 tons. Typical sauropods probably held their necks and tails horizontally or at a slight slope, but brachiosaurs were specially built to reach upward into trees. When fully grown, they could reach twice as high as a giraffe. With their heads in the treetops, they used their teeth like a rake to tear off mouthfuls of leaves.

 ❯ Sauropod fossils and footprints have been found on every continent except Antarctica.

araucaria leaves were hard and often ended in sharp points

Head for heights

In this scene from the late Jurassic Period, about 160 million years ago, a herd of brachiosaurs are feeding on araucaria trees. Unlike other sauropods, brachiosaurs had extralarge front legs, which contributed to their 40-ft. (12-m) height. Paleontologists once believed that brachiosaurs waded deep into water because fossils seem to show that their nostrils were high on their heads. This is now thought unlikely because the water pressure would have prevented their lungs from working.

The large front legs gave brachiosaurs high shoulders and a sloping back.

Stomach stones

Instead of chewing, many dinosaurs swallowed stones to help them digest food. The stones, called gastroliths, lodged in a dinosaur's stomach, where they ground up the food after it had been swallowed. These gastroliths were found near a sauropod's ribcage in New Mexico. They have been worn smooth through use.

⊖ DINOSAUR DROPPINGS

Large dinosaurs had to eat an enormous amount of food to keep themselves alive. Their droppings were equally impressive, and they sometimes fossilized. Fossils like these, known as coprolites, can be more than 24 in. (60cm) long. Looked at under a microscope, a coprolite often reveals ancient fragments of plants or bone, giving some idea of the kind of dinosaur that left it behind.

fossilized dinosaur droppings probably made by a sauropod called *Titanosaurus*

mature adults formed
a barrier between the
predators and the
herd's young

Deinonychus

Deinonychus *was far
smaller than* Iguanodon
*but had a saberlike claw
on each hind foot*

Iguanodon

LIFE IN A HERD

Despite their size, plant-eating dinosaurs lived in a world full
of danger, where predators could attack at any time. To protect
themselves, many herbivores lived in herds. They fed and traveled
together and raised their young in the safety of a group. By keeping
close to one another, they made it harder for predators to single out one
from the crowd. However, life in a herd could sometimes be dangerous.
Occasionally entire herds died when disasters suddenly wiped them out.

Iguanodon *moved on
its back feet when
running, with its front
legs off the ground*

> *Iguanodon* was named for its teeth, which look like large versions of an iguana's (a plant-eating lizard).

◒ DEADLY TRAP

Iguanodon was discovered in 1822, making it one of the first dinosaurs to be studied by scientists. At first, its thumb spike caused confusion—an early drawing showed the spike on *Iguanodon*'s nose! This mistake was later corrected. In 1878, coal miners at Bernissart, Belgium, discovered an entire herd of *Iguanodon* buried underground. The dinosaurs had fallen into a ravine and were slowly fossilized inside seams of coal.

drawing showing thumb spike on *Iguanodon*'s nose

Closing ranks

In early Cretaceous Period forests, a herd of *Iguanodon* senses trouble in the air. The dinosaurs are being pursued by a pack of *Deinonychus*, and they are preparing for a possible attack. The adults have positioned themselves around their vulnerable young and are doing their best to stage an orderly retreat. If the attack comes, the adult *Iguanodon* will fight back using the lethal spikes that they have on their thumbs.

thumb was armed with a long, sharply pointed spike

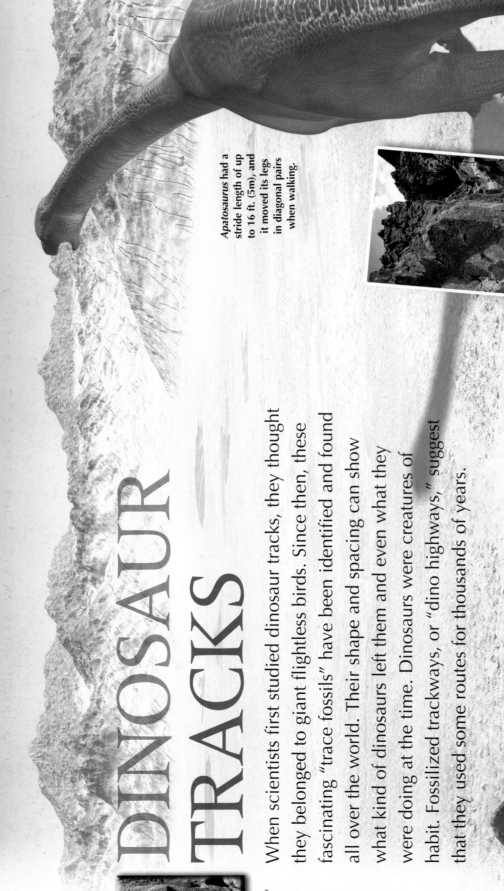

DINOSAUR TRACKS

When scientists first studied dinosaur tracks, they thought they belonged to giant flightless birds. Since then, these fascinating "trace fossils" have been identified and found all over the world. Their shape and spacing can show what kind of dinosaurs left them and even what they were doing at the time. Dinosaurs were creatures of habit. Fossilized trackways, or "dino highways," suggest that they used some routes for thousands of years.

Apatosaurus had a stride length of up to 16 ft. (5m), and it moved its legs in diagonal pairs when walking.

Sauropod prints are deep and round. The rear feet left claw marks, but the front ones often did not.

Vertical tracks

Just like fossilized bones, fossilized tracks often change position after they have formed. The tracks shown here, in northern Argentina, were left by a theropod striding across an ancient shoreline. Over millions of years, earth movements slowly tipped them up on edge. A geologist standing beneath them shows their scale.

Gallimimus could probably run more than 30 mph (50km/h) in short bursts.

Gallimimus and other theropods (meat eaters) left three-toed prints.

> TRACE FOSSIL—*preserved remains that show how animals lived*

Traces in time

Walking across the bed of a desert lake, three different dinosaurs leave distinctive tracks in the rapidly drying mud. Like all sauropods, *Apatosaurus* had soles shaped like giant pancakes, leaving rounded tracks, often with little sign of claws. *Gallimimus* and *Dryosaurus* left three-toed prints, like the first dinosaur tracks to be found. The faster they ran, the deeper their toes dug into the mud.

When running, Dryosaurus's three-toed prints were spaced far apart.

Unusually for a plant eater, *Dryosaurus* had short hands and ran on its back legs.

"... footprints are those of creatures in the full tide of life."

Richard Swann Lull (1867–1957)
U.S. paleontologist and track expert

● FOSSILIZATION

To fossilize, tracks first have to harden by drying in the sun. Next, they are gently flooded with water, which buries them in layers of sediment. As the sediment builds up, increasing pressure slowly turns it into rock. After millions of years, the rock is exposed to the air, and it begins to erode. Finally, the fossil tracks appear at the surface. With luck, the tracks are spotted before they eventually crumble away.

1. Footprint makes an impression in mud

2. Footprint fills up with more mud

3. Over millions of years, the mud turns to rock

4. Material filling the impression washes out, leaving a fossilized track

〉 In 2009, fossil hunters in France found sauropod tracks almost 6.5 ft. (2m) across—the biggest ever discovered.

www.amnh.org/exhibitions/dinosaurs/trackways/

Whip crack!

Diplodocus had nearly 80 vertebrae in its tail, which had a very long, slender tip. It may have been able to crack it like a whip, breaking the speed of sound. The cracking sound would have warned away predators and may have helped *Diplodocus* stay in touch with its own kind.

Trumpeting crest

Parasaurolophus had the largest crest of any hadrosaur, measuring up to 6 ft. (1.8m) long. Using X-ray scanners, scientists have found that it contained hollow tubes linking the dinosaur's nostrils with the back of its throat. When *Parasaurolophus* breathed through its crest, these long tubes may have made the air reverberate, producing loud bellowing or trumpeting sounds.

crest formed by enlarged upper jaw and nasal bones

incoming air entered the crest from the nostrils

CALL OF THE WILD

Today's reptiles are mostly silent except for the sounds they make when they move. But over 65 million years ago, the world's landscapes may have echoed with the eerie noises of hadrosaurs, or duck-billed dinosaurs. Many hadrosaurs had large crests on the tops of their heads. Some of these crests were hollow, turning them into echo chambers that might have worked like enormous trombones.

"It's the kind of sound that would easily be heard by other animals through a thick rain forest."

Tom Williamson
paleontologist, describing a computer-generated reconstruction of Parasaurolophus's call

> Hadrosaurs have been nicknamed the "cows of the Cretaceous" because they formed huge plant-eating herds.

air reverberated as it traveled
through the crest, which may have
created loud, trumpeting sounds

tubes doubled back
at the tip of the crest

air flowed out
of the crest to
the lungs

crest contained
several tubelike
channels linked to
other internal spaces

www.cnn.com/TECH/9712/05/dino.speaks/

⊜ FAMILY CRESTS

Edmontosaurus had a long, low skull—a shape shared by
Maiasaura and several other hadrosaurs—but many of the
hadrosaur family had conspicuous crests. *Lambeosaurus* had
a crest shaped like a hatchet, with an upward-pointing blade,
while *Corythosaurus* had one that looked like a helmet,
flattened on either side. Hadrosaurs fed on plants. They tore
off mouthfuls of food with their "beaks" and then chewed
them with a battery of teeth at the back of their jaws.

Edmontosaurus   **Lambeosaurus**   **Corythosaurus**

NERVOUS SYSTEM—a body system that works like wiring, letting animals sense their surroundings and move

BRAINS AND SENSES

For their size, dinosaurs often had tiny brains. But this did not mean they were stupid, because keen senses helped them survive. Plant eaters used sight and smell to find their food. While they were feeding, their eyes and ears alerted them if anything dangerous was nearby. Fast-moving hunters such as *Troodon* had relatively large brains and found their food mostly by sight. They were experts at spotting movement but probably not so good at noticing prey that stood still.

Crunch!

Pachycephalosaurs had dome-shaped brain cases up to 8 in. (20cm) thick. At one time, scientists thought that the males used them in head-butting contests during the breeding season. However, pachycephalosaurs did not have reinforced necks, so it is more likely that they swung their heads into each other's sides, like male giraffes do today.

⊜ BRAIN POWER

In relation to their bodies, stegosaurs had the smallest brains of all dinosaurs, measuring only a few millionths of their total body weight. Stegosaurs had an extra "mini brain," or ganglion, above their hips to control their back legs and tail. Theropods were more intelligent, although the biggest still had minuscule brains for their size. *Troodon* and its relatives were probably head of the class in dinosaur intelligence because their brains were well developed and their bodies relatively small.

ganglion controlled back legs and tail

Stegosaurus

> *Stegosaurus*'s brain weighed about 2.6 oz. (75g)—about the same as a large chicken's egg.

fluid-filled semicircular canals sensed movement and created the sense of balance

slit-shaped pupils would have helped Troodon to spot horizontal movement in bright daylight; at night, they would have opened wide

nostrils carried air over sensory cells above the roof of the mouth and were able to open and close

olfactory lobes at the front of the brain managed the sense of smell

ear opened through a simple hole in the skull

Quick-witted hunter

Troodon was only about 6.5 ft. (2m) long, but it belonged to a group of advanced theropods that had unusually well-developed brains. It was probably warm-blooded, which would have enabled the whole of its nervous system to work at high speed. The shape of its brain case shows that it had a fairly good sense of smell, but its most important sense was sight. Because its eyes were so large, some experts think it may have hunted at night.

like most dinosaurs, Troodon *may have had a poor sense of taste*

EGG MOUNTAIN

INCUBATE—to keep an egg warm so that the embryo inside can develop

Dinosaurs bred by laying eggs, like most reptiles do today. Some of their eggs were not much larger than a chicken's, but the biggest—belonging to sauropods—were more than 16 in. (40cm) long. At Egg Mountain, in Montana, an entire herd of duck-billed dinosaurs nested together. Fossils show that the parent dinosaurs took care of their eggs and also collected food for the newly hatched young.

Family group

Alerted by their cheeping, a female *Maiasaura* tends her eggs and young. These dinosaurs made bowl-shaped nests and lined them with plants, which helped keep the eggs warm. Fossils show that the young were poorly developed when they hatched—a sign that they were fed by their parents.

females nested at the same time, making it harder for predators to reach the eggs or young

⊖ LONG DROP

Small and medium-size dinosaurs could squat to lay their eggs, but giant sauropods—such as *Apatosaurus*—could hardly bend their back legs. Their eggs faced a daunting drop of 6.5 ft. (2m) or more before they hit the ground. To stop them from breaking, female sauropods may have had a fleshy egg-laying tube, or ovipositor. Because the tube was soft, it would not have fossilized, so none has ever been found.

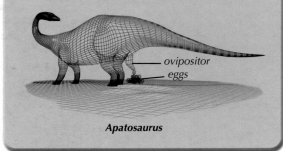

ovipositor
eggs

Apatosaurus

Nesting styles

This fossilized nest from China was constructed by a predatory theropod toward the end of the Dinosaur Age. It contains 22 elongated eggs, arranged in a circle. Many of the eggs have broken shells, revealing tiny dinosaur skeletons inside. Not all dinosaurs were this neat—sauropods laid their eggs in rather messy piles.

plants created heat as they rotted, incubating the eggs

 ▷ For their size, the biggest dinosaurs laid small eggs, equivalent to a tiny fraction of their own weight.

nests were neatly
spaced out in the
breeding colony

nest made from
soil scraped
into a ring

eggs laid
in a circle

young probably
remained in the nest
for several weeks

mature embryo curled
up inside an egg

PACK ATTACK

Plant-eating dinosaurs weren't the only ones that often lived in groups. Some fast, quick-witted killers worked like wolves in a pack, singling out prey many times their own size. One of these was *Deinonychus*—a predator that used extralarge hind claws to attack its victims. Measuring about 10 ft. (3m) long, *Deinonychus* was light enough to leap aboard its prey. It then set to work with its claws, bringing much bigger dinosaurs crashing to the ground.

Winning formula

Small pack-hunting killers lived throughout the Dinosaur Age. One of the earliest was *Coelophysis*. At Ghost Ranch, in New Mexico, thousands of *Coelophysis* fossils have been found together. The fossils come in two sizes—scientists think that the larger ones are males.

Deinonychus

hands had three fingers, tipped with long claws

One against many

In a forest clearing, about 100 million years ago, a plant-eating *Tenontosaurus* is fighting for its life as a pack of *Deinonychus* slash at it with their claws. Unlike early dinosaurs, *Deinonychus* was probably warm-blooded. A covering of feathers would have kept in its body heat, enabling it to stay active even in cold conditions. Warm-blooded animals make effective hunters, but they need more fuel than cold-blooded ones to keep their bodies working. As a result, the *Deinonychus* pack would be constantly on the hunt.

> *Deinonychus*'s sickle-shaped rear claws were about 5 in. (12cm) long.

second toe swiveled
downward when
Deinonychus *attacked*

Tenontosaurus

extralarge claw on second
toe stayed off the ground
when Deinonychus *was on
the move, keeping it sharp*

huge rear leg muscles braced Tyrannosaurus rex while it fed

skin may have had scattered feathers

Tower of strength

With teeth measuring up to 12 in. (30cm) long, *Tyrannosaurus rex* had a "bite and tear" feeding technique that made short work of fallen flesh. Unlike many predatory dinosaurs, its upper jaw ended in a blunt, U-shaped snout. This enabled it to tear off up to 165 lbs. (75kg) of food at time—about the same weight as an average man. It towered over its food on its colossal back legs, while its tiny front legs hung in the air. For a dinosaur, its sense of smell was unusually good, helping it track down dead food.

large openings between skull bones helped reduce the weight of the head

> **SCAVENGER**—*an animal that feeds mainly or entirely on dead remains*

DEATH ON TWO LEGS

Tyrannosaurus rex is the world's most famous predator, even though it vanished over 65 million years ago. We know exactly what it looked like thanks to some incredible fossil finds. One of them, nicknamed "Sue," is amazingly well preserved—a sign that it was covered by mud or sand just after it died. But *Tyrannosaurus rex*'s lifestyle remains a puzzle. Instead of being a serial killer, it may have gotten some or all of its food by scavenging from dead remains.

teeth at front of jaw had a backward curve and a D-shaped cross section

KILLERS COMPARED

Tyrannosaurus rex weighed up to 7.5 tons and measured up to 43 ft. (13m) from head to tail. Despite this, it was probably not the largest land predator of all time. *Carcharodontosaurus* may have weighed over 11 tons, while *Giganotosaurus* tipped the scales at over 13 tons. The longest of all may have been *Spinosaurus*—a sail-backed hunter with jaws like a crocodile's that is thought to have fed on fish. It may have been up to 60 ft. (18m) long.

Spinosaurus

Carcharodontosaurus

Giganotosaurus

❯ In 2009, paleontologists identified a miniature tyrannosaur, called *Raptorex*. It weighed only a hundredth as much as *Tyrannosaurus rex*.

FIGHTING BACK

OSTEODERM—a large, raised scale that is reinforced by a layer of bone

For plant-eating dinosaurs, survival meant being permanently on guard. If they were attacked, very few could use their teeth as weapons. Instead, some hit back by rearing up on their back legs or by stabbing their opponents with sharp claws. *Ankylosaurus* had some of the best protection of all. The dinosaur was covered in armor plating, and its stiff tail ended in a massive club that could smash an enemy's skull.

Deadly spikes

Stegosaurus had bony plates on its back, but its real weapons were vicious spikes on its sides and at the tip of its tail. The spikes pointed outward, so they stabbed into an enemy as *Stegosaurus* swung around.

tail spikes

Killer blow

With its 5.5-ton body and superb defenses, *Ankylosaurus* was built to stand and fight rather than to run away. Here, the dinosaur is fending off an *Albertosaurus* that has unwisely closed in to attack. *Ankylosaurus*'s skin was reinforced and protected with bony plates, or osteoderms, and its tail club could swing with shattering force if anything came too close. Its only weak point was its underside, which had unarmored skin.

bony plates protected each eye

Ankylosaurus

⊖ REARING UP

Sauropods had legs like pillars and spent almost all of their time on all fours. However, faced with danger, some could rear up on their back legs in a bid to trample an attacker. Many kinds, including *Barosaurus*, had a large claw on the inside of each front foot that could have ripped downward into an attacker. However, rearing up could put the huge animal off balance, sending it crashing to the ground.

Barosaurus rearing up

> Ankylosaur body armor was so strong that if these dinosaurs were around today, they would be bulletproof.

skin is protected
by bony plates
and knobs, or
osteoderms

tail club had two
large lobes and
weighed more than
110 lb. (50kg)

Albertosaurus

rows of extralarge
plates ran along
its back and sides

Scissorhands

Therizinosaurus had the longest
claws ever known—they could
be almost 3 ft. (1m) long. They
might have worked as weapons,
but their main job was probably
gathering plants for food.

MORTAL COMBAT

In 1971, fossil hunters in Mongolia made the find of the century: two dinosaurs locked in combat. One of them was *Velociraptor*, a fast-moving predator. The other was *Protoceratops*—a 5-ft. (1.5-m)-long plant eater with jaws like a beak. The two animals were evenly matched, but something brought the fight to a sudden end. The most likely explanation is that a collapsing cliff smothered them in sand. More than 75 million years later, the fossil fighters are still locked together in their deadly embrace.

"... collapsing in death, the two bodies were covered by blowing sand before scavengers could find the bodies and tear them apart."

David Spalding
geologist based in Canada

Protoceratops was one of the first ceratopsians—a group of dinosaurs that evolved spectacular frills and enormous horns.

1. *Protoceratops stands its ground as Velociraptor approaches—perhaps because it was guarding its nest and eggs.*

2. *Protoceratops lunges forward to defend itself, while Velociraptor tries to lash out with the killer claws on its back feet.*

Robber cousins

Velociraptor was discovered in 1922 during a U.S. expedition to Mongolia. Its name means "fast robber," and it was very quick on its feet. *Velociraptor* was closely related to *Deinonychus* and may also have been warm-blooded.

> **FRILL**—*a shieldlike extension of the skull that sweeps backward, protecting the neck*

3. With one of its front legs trapped by *Protoceratops*'s beak, *Velociraptor* falls on its side, kicking at its enemy's neck and underside.

The fossil shows the two dinosaurs locked together in their fight.

FLAMING CLIFFS

The fighting dinosaurs were found in a part of the Gobi Desert called the Flaming Cliffs. This remote desert landscape is where *Protoceratops* was discovered in 1922. A year later, another expedition made a find almost as famous as the fighting dinosaurs—an adult *Oviraptor* sitting on its eggs.

one of the world's great fossil-hunting regions

Fatal encounter

Compared with *Velociraptor*, *Protoceratops* was slow moving, which made it an easy target. However, its skull was armored with a protective frill, and it could inflict bone-crushing injuries with its bite. *Velociraptor* was equipped with a lethal claw on each foot, but in this fight they may have led to its downfall. One of them became caught in *Protoceratops*'s neck, ensuring that *Velociraptor* was also buried by sand.

> *Velociraptor* may have had a covering of feathers, like many other small theropod dinosaurs.

MINIMIZING WEIGHT

Ceratopsians' head shields, or frills, could be twice the size of a car door. *Triceratops*'s frill was made of solid bone, which meant that it was extremely heavy. Many of its relatives minimized weight by having frills with large gaps in the bone that were covered by skin. *Styracosaurus* had two gaps, and its frill was edged with horns and spikes. Even so, the animal still weighed 3 tons.

Styracosaurus's skull with frill

older teeth were continually replaced by new ones underneath

RHINO DINOSAURS

With its three horns and its gigantic head shield or frill, *Triceratops* was one of the most distinctive plant eaters from the end of the Dinosaur Age. It weighed up to 7 tons, and its skull was one of the biggest ever grown by a land animal, with a maximum length of over 8 ft. (2.5m). Like other ceratopsians, or "rhino dinos," it used its horns against predators, but males probably turned them against their rivals when the time came to breed.

Giant head

This fossilized skeleton, found in Alberta, Canada, shows the huge proportions of *Triceratops*'s skull. The skull took up about a third of its total body length. It had three horns, up to 3 ft. (1m) long, and jaws that ended in a beak. The beak was covered by a layer of horn, just like a bird's.

> Ceratopsians may have been able to signal to each other by "blushing" the skin covering their frills.

Locking horns

Straining with all their might, two male *Triceratops* struggle for supremacy during the breeding season. In contests like these, rival males would probably have rammed or bulldozed their opponents rather than trying to inflict injuries with their horns. However, these ritual battles could take a vicious turn: some fossil skulls show serious gouges where horns hit home.

FISHING DINOSAURS

Dinosaurs were land animals, and almost all the carnivorous kinds hunted land-dwelling prey. *Baryonyx* was different. Although it was a land-dwelling predator, it lurked by the sides of rivers and lakes, ready to seize fish that swam within range. As soon as a fish was close enough, it would plunge its jaws beneath the surface or hook it with its front claws. Within seconds, the wriggling fish would be hauled onto land, often to be swallowed whole.

Sudden death

Baryonyx had jaws like a crocodile's, with almost 100 conical, sharply pointed teeth set in a narrow snout that widened toward the tip. It caught small fish with its teeth alone, but for bigger fish it used its claws. Measuring over 12 in. (30cm) long, the claws stabbed fish and then swept them out of the water and onto dry land. Fossilized fish scales have been found with *Baryonyx* remains, along with bones from smaller dinosaurs.

bulbous snout is typical of fish-eating reptiles, including today's crocodiles and gharials

> **SPINOSAUR**—*a predatory dinosaur with narrow jaws and simple, conical teeth*

catfish often
live in shallow,
slow-moving
water, making
them easy prey

teeth had a
simple shape but
extremely deep
roots, with up to
half their total
length buried
in the jaw

Lucky find

Baryonyx was found by an amateur fossil hunter in 1983. He spotted one of its claws in a clay pit in southern England—the site of a river estuary when *Baryonyx* was alive. An excavation then uncovered most of its skeleton. It had lain undisturbed for more than 125 million years.

● SAIL-BACKED DINOSAURS

Baryonyx belonged to a group of hunters with highly specialized jaws. Its best-known relative is *Spinosaurus*—a colossal predator up to 60 ft. (18m) long. Unlike *Baryonyx*, *Spinosaurus* had a giant sail along its back, held up by a row of bony spines. The tallest spines, halfway down its back, were higher than an adult man. *Spinosaurus* may have used its sail to soak up warmth from the sunshine or in breeding-season displays.

Spinosaurus

❯ *Baryonyx* was about 30 ft. (9m) long. Another fish-eating spinosaur, called *Suchomimus*, measured up to 40 ft. (12m).

Early bird

The world's oldest fossil of a true bird was found in Germany in 1861. Called *Archaeopteryx*, it had teeth, clawed wings, and a long, bony tail. It looked like a small theropod dinosaur, but it had feathers and could fly. *Archaeopteryx* lived about 150 million years ago—earlier than many dino-birds.

outstretched arms worked as stabilizers and helped sweep insects toward Caudipteryx's jaws

DINO-BIRDS

In the past 20 years, scientists have made some amazing discoveries in the quarries of northeast China. As well as ancient plants and mammals, they have found fossils of feathered dinosaurs. The earliest kinds had short and simple feathers, which worked like a coat of fur. But over millions of years, their feathers became stronger and more like the flight feathers that birds have today. Eventually, dino-birds evolved working wings, and true birds were born.

 Fossils of dino-birds are often found in ancient volcanic ash, which preserves the outline of feathers.

⊝ FOUR-WINGED FLIERS

No one knows how dino-birds started to fly. They may have begun by gliding onto their prey from trees, or they may have jumped up from the ground. Wings could also be useful when running up slopes, which is how some ground-dwelling birds use them today. Most dino-birds used their arms as wings, but some kinds—such as *Microraptor*—also had long feathers on their legs and may have flown with all fours. These four-winged fliers eventually died out, leaving two-winged species that evolved into birds.

Microraptor

tail had a large fan of feathers at the tip

Caudipteryx

birdlike beak had a small number of simple teeth in the upper jaw

High-speed chase

Swerving after a dragonfly, *Caudipteryx* stretches out its feathered arms as it closes in on its prey. It could not fly, but its feathered arms and tail helped it steer. Its body was covered with an insulating layer of short down feathers. They would have kept its body at a warm and steady temperature—a feature shared by all birds alive today. Fossils of *Caudipteryx* were discovered in the late 1990s. They date back to the early Cretaceous Period, about 125 million years ago.

Undersea evidence
In the late 1970s, oil prospectors found a huge depression on the seabed off the coast of Mexico. Known as the Chicxulub crater, it is probably the place where the meteorite struck Earth, ending the Dinosaur Age. The crater is almost 125 mi. (200km) across.

As well as dinosaurs, the great extinction swept away flying reptiles, or pterosaurs, and many of the reptiles that lived in the sea.

FATAL IMPACT

Throughout the Dinosaur Age, new kinds of dinosaurs slowly evolved, and old ones gradually became extinct. But 65 million years ago, something catastrophic happened. All the dinosaurs vanished, together with many other kinds of animal life. This worldwide disaster came from outer space, when an enormous meteorite collided with Earth. The meteorite was destroyed during the impact, releasing as much energy as a billion atomic bombs.

Living dinosaurs
Most people would not confuse a bird with a dinosaur, but beneath their feathers, birds are dinosaurs in disguise. Scientists even classify them as dinosaurs because they are direct descendants of dino-birds.

Alamosaurus

World on fire
Within hours of the meteorite impact, a deadly combination of shock waves and heat swept Earth. Blasted high into the atmosphere, billions of tons of dust encircled the planet, killing plant life by blocking the sunshine. Without food, plant-eating dinosaurs soon died, and large predators followed. The animal world would never be the same again.

> The meteorite that ended the Dinosaur Age was probably traveling at over 43,500 mph (70,000km/h).

"... suddenly you're dealing with an animal that isn't extinct anymore. The dinosaurs are still alive."

Philip J. Currie
Canadian paleontologist and expert on the origin of birds

Large dinosaurs were particularly vulnerable to disasters because they could not take cover and needed enormous amounts of food.

Triceratops

⊖ SURVIVORS

The meteorite impact ended the Cretaceous Period and brought the reign of the reptiles to a close. But amid the devastation, birds, mammals, and some reptiles managed to survive. The biggest surviving reptiles were crocodiles, which managed to live by scavenging food from dead remains. Reptile survivors also included the ancestors of today's snakes and lizards, as well as tuataras, which belong to a group of reptiles as old as the earliest dinosaurs.

tortoise

tuatara

cobra

crocodile

http://paleobiology.si.edu/blastPast/index.html

Tyrannosaurus rex

GLOSSARY

asymmetrical
Having a lopsided shape. Asymmetrical flight feathers are a key feature of birds, separating them from feathered dinosaurs.

camouflage
Shapes and colors that help an animal blend in with its background so that it can hide from its enemies or get close to its prey.

carnivorous
Eating animals as food.

ceratopsian
A plant-eating dinosaur with a body like a rhinoceros, horns, and a bony head shield or frill.

cold-blooded
Describes an animal whose body temperature goes up and down in step with the temperature outside. Today's reptiles are all cold-blooded, but some dinosaurs may have been warm-blooded instead.

crater
A circular hollow created by a volcanic eruption or by a meteorite hitting Earth.

down
A layer of short, fluffy feathers that feathered dinosaurs used to keep warm.

erode
To gradually wear away. Rocks are eroded mainly by wind and rain, and also by frost splitting them apart.

evolution
Slow changes that make living things better at survival. Evolution happens over many generations, instead of during a single lifetime. It gradually alters the way animals look and lets them develop new ways of life.

evolve
To change through evolution.

excavation
A careful dig designed to reveal fossils buried in the ground.

extinct
No longer living anywhere on Earth. Extinction can happen gradually or in bursts that wipe out many forms of life at the same time.

flight feather
A long feather with a lopsided shape. Flight feathers keep birds airborne when they beat their wings.

fossil
Remains of living things that have been preserved in the ground. In most fossils, the original remains are replaced by hard minerals, which can keep their shape for millions of years.

hadrosaur
A plant-eating dinosaur with a ducklike beak and often a bony crest on its skull.

herbivore
Any animal that eats plants.

incubate
To keep eggs warm by sitting on them. Birds incubate their eggs and so did small warm-blooded dinosaurs.

insulating
Slowing down heat loss so that something stays warm.

lift
A natural resistance to the pull of gravity that keeps a flying animal in the air.

mammal
An animal that has fur and that feeds its young on milk. Unlike reptiles, almost all mammals give birth to live young.

meteorite
A rock from space that penetrates the atmosphere and hits Earth's surface.

paleontologist
A scientist who studies prehistoric life using fossils and other kinds of evidence.

pigments
Colored chemicals that are found in rocks and in living things.

prehistoric
Describes something that existed before recorded history began.

preservation
In nature, anything that makes dead remains keep their shape.

prey
Animals that are hunted by others as food. Plant-eating dinosaurs were prey animals, but so were many predatory dinosaurs because they were hunted by dinosaurs larger than themselves.

pterosaur
A reptile that flew on wings made of skin. Pterosaurs were not dinosaurs, but they lived alongside them.

reptile
An animal with scaly skin that lays eggs or gives birth to live young. Reptiles include snakes, lizards, tortoises, and crocodiles, as well as dinosaurs.

sauropod
A plant-eating dinosaur with a huge body and a very long neck and tail. Sauropods included the largest land animals that have ever lived.

scavenger
An animal that feeds on dead remains.

sediment
Small particles of mud or grit that settle out of water.

semicircular canal
A fluid-filled space inside an animal's head that detects movement and the pull of gravity.

species
A group of living things that look like each other and that breed only with their own kind.

spinosaur
A predatory dinosaur with narrow jaws, like a crocodile's, and sometimes a bony crest running down its back.

theropod
A dinosaur with small arms and hollow bones that walked upright on its back legs. Most theropods were predators, although some fed on a mix of plant and animal food.

vertebra (pl. vertebrae)
An individual bone in the spinal column (or backbone) of an animal.

warm-blooded
Describes an animal that stays warm even when the temperature outside is cold.

INDEX

INVESTIGATE

The skull of a *Tarbosaurus* from the Gobi Desert—one of hundreds of dinosaur exhibits at the Natural History Museum in London, England.

Find out more about dinosaurs and prehistoric life by visiting museums and fossil-hunting sites or by watching and reading about these awe-inspiring animals in documentaries, movies, and reference books.

Museums and exhibitions

Most of the world's greatest dinosaur fossils are displayed in museums, giving you a chance to come face to face with these giants from the past.

📖 *The Dinosaur Hunters* by Lowell Dingus and Mark Norell (Andre Deutsch)

◈ American Museum of Natural History, Central Park West at 79th Street, New York, NY 10024

⬤ http://paleobiology.si.edu/dinosaurs/collection/where/main.html

A fossil ammonite from southern England's Jurassic Coast, where crumbling rock exposes new fossils every year.

Fossil-hunting sites

You can hunt for fossils in your local area. Try hunting at rocky places inland or on the shore. Head for areas that have sedimentary (layered) rocks. If you are on the coast, stay away from cliffs and keep a check on the tide.

📖 *KFK Rocks and Fossils* by Margaret Hynes (Kingfisher)

◈ The Dinosaur Diamond Prehistoric Highway in Colorado and Utah is famous for its expert excavation sites and museums.

⬤ www.sdnhm.org/kids/fossils/ffwhere.html and www.wyodino.org

Animation brings the past to life in this stunning model of *Torosaurus*, a horned dinosaur, built to appear in movies.

Documentaries and movies

You can't visit the Dinosaur Age, but thanks to computerized animation, documentaries, and movies, the distant past can seem amazingly real.

Chinese paleontologist Xu Xing carefully extracts a fossil in the Gobi Desert, one of many exciting discoveries he has described in scientific magazines.

📀 *Walking With Dinosaurs* (BBC Warner)

◈ *Dinosaurs Alive!* at some IMAX and other giant-screen theaters

⬤ http://dsc.discovery.com/dinosaurs and www.bbc.co.uk/sn/prehistoric_life/dinosaurs

Books and magazines

If you are fascinated by dinosaurs and other prehistoric animals, it's hard to beat illustrated reference books. Many magazines contain up-to-the-minute news about dinosaur discoveries.

📖 *The Kingfisher Dinosaur Encyclopedia* by Michael Benton (Kingfisher)

◈ Visit your local library to discover a whole range of dinosaur books.

⬤ www.nationalgeographic.com